Believe smile Create Inspire

Invent Blossom Publicize

Motivate Grow Giggle

Think Succeed sell

celebrate Brainstorm Adapt

Learn share Save Plan

Maddie Bradshaw's

You Can Start a Business, Too!

by Maddie with lots of help from Mom & Margot

published by

m3 girl designs

creators of
"the original, interchangeable bottle cap necklace"®

Please visit our Web site at M3GirlDesigns.com

Printed in USA

Library of Congress Control Number
2010934457

ISBN 978-0-615-38758-1

For my Dad:

Thank you for always being there for me, guiding me, and supporting me throughout the years.

And for my Mom:

Thank you for helping build the business to where it is today and encouraging me to never give up.

Love you both, Maddie

Awesome ideas
are ready to blossom
inside each of us.

Every girl is filled with unique ideas. And from the simplest idea, wonderful things can happen. When I was only ten, I thought up Snap Caps®, and with encouragement and guidance from my parents, I was able to turn my dream into a real company.

You, too, have the potential to start your own business. Remember to follow your dreams, and make sure work is also fun. Creating Snap Caps® has been a great experience because it allows me to draw and do what I love, while earning money at the same time. So be sure whatever you decide to do is your passion. As long as you're happy, your great ideas will be successful!

Maddie Bradshaw

My first cap design featured **Albert Einstein**, an incredibly smart scientist who was born long, long ago in 1879. I  admire him because of his brilliance. He looked pretty cool as a decoration on my school locker. Best of all, he was a man who came up with his own amazing *ideas!*

And when my favorite toy store
sold my first batch of
Snap Caps® in no
time at all,

...in just 2 hours!
Can you believe it?

my business
officially started.

"Here I am, dreaming about
starting a business."
Me and my Dad, David

"Our dog Annie puts a
smile on everyone's face."
My Mom, Diane

"Fashion and trends are my
sister Margot's specialty.
Just ask her!"
My little sister, Margot

If you want to be an

ENTREPRENEUR,

*it helps to know what
the word means.*

Definition

entrepreneur
Someone (just like you)
who organizes and manages
a business venture.

It's actually a fancy French word
that sounds quite impressive. Try this:
Hold your head up high and say out
loud with a little dramatic flourish,
"entrepreneur" (on-trah-pre-noor).
Wow, I bet you feel the excitement
of success already!

The Best Business Ideas Start with

YOU

PERSONALITY PROFILE
What makes you the happiest?
What excites you the most?
Are you a busy bee who likes being active?
Or do you prefer quiet activities at home?
Do you enjoy talking to new people?
Are you kind of shy?
Are you always thinking of new ways to do things?
Do you have goals for the future?
How good is your sense of humor?
Are you a team player?
Do you stick to plans?
Or do you like being spontaneous?

Fashion might be your passion
Share your flair!

- Design a bunch of really fun patches for backpacks and clothes.
- Make fabulous scarves out of colorful felt.
- Shoot a fashion forecast video for girls every season and post it on YouTube.
- Design a collection of doll's clothes.
- Start a hair-braiding business.

Animals might make you smile
Pedigreed projects for everyone.

- Got a fenced-in backyard? Create a summertime doggy playground.
- Instead of just walking dogs, add in a canine fitness program.
- Cats are independent, but they still love company—be a friendly kitty sitter.
- Organize a pet beauty pageant and bring in sponsors.
- Paint pet portraits with tons of personality.
- Make custom paw-print tree ornaments.

Sports could be your dream

Be an entrepreneurial champ, on or off the team.

- Organize a mini-triathlon for kids your age.
- Create pom-poms for sneakers in school team colors.
- Design flower-power bike baskets and awesome stickers for helmets.
- Lead a fitness bootcamp once a week in your local park.
- Write a sports Web site just for girls.
- Design a collection of hand-painted soccer shoelaces.

Maybe cooking is your calling

Sample these yummy ideas.

- Re-invent the brownie, making them into delicious one-bite pops.
- Film a series of kid-friendly cooking videos to post on YouTube or on your Web site.
- Devise a cookie-of-the-month club, outdoing yourself with fascinating flavors.
- Make up an inventive fresh fruit ice cream topping.
- Do something amazing with popcorn...give every flavor a fun name.
- Have international food parties just for kids...introducing them to new tastes.
- Become the Veggie Princess, inventing a vegetable snack just for kids.

There's an artist in everyone
Where will your talents take you?

- Draw a comic strip.
- Make decorations out of found objects and broken bits of pottery.
- Draw 10-minute portraits at local fairs and events.
- Organize community art shows.
- Paint wall murals in kid's bedrooms.

Are you a natural-born entertainer?
Go ahead, make them smile!

- Develop a musical magic act for kid's parties.
- Write a 10-minute play and produce it with all-kid performers.
- Create a weekly kid's radio show.
- Write movie reviews for your Web site.
- Become a party planner.
- Organize a talent camp and put on a show!

How about home chores?
There's always a better way to do things.

- Become a closet organizer.
- Help kids organize their school lockers.
- Start a leaf-raking business.
- Mow lawns.
- Grow different types of herbs and sell them.
- Paint outdoor furniture.
- Help neighbors set up garage sales.

Share your computer smarts
You're never too young (or old) to start

- Help kids create a basic Web site.
- Show kids how to write and design an online storybook.
- Help friends download pictures to make an amazing scrapbook.
- Introduce older people to computer basics.
- Film your grandparents or your friend's grandparents as they talk about their life...then make a DVD.

Are you eco-friendly?
Green goes with everything.

- Design green-power t-shirts and accessories.
- Create YouTube videos about saving the planet.
- Create a solar-panel backpack that can charge an iPod.
- Organize a "Planet-Saving" workshop for your friends.
- Set up a swapping club for clothes, books, and DVDs.
- Teach people how to compost.

Think of ways to have fun with kids
You're full of inspiring ideas.

- Organize singalongs.
- Babysit with style.
- Create a summertime arts-and-crafts camp.
- Help little kids learn to ice skate.
- Set up a beauty parlor for dolls.
- Start a kid's gardening class.
- Invent a puppet show...and sell your puppets.

Grandparents need a helping hand, too
You'll help…you'll learn.

- Plant flowers and assist with all sorts of garden chores.
- Accompany seniors to the supermarket.
- Share a weekly hour of good cheer.
- Make photo albums out of priceless old pictures.
- Become the world's best home-chore helper.

Spread some holiday cheer
There's no better gift.

- Sell mistletoe bouquets decorated with feathers and beads.
- Make fancy Easter eggs.
- Sell hand-painted pumpkins.
- Create tree ornaments from the shells you gathered all summer.
- Bake Fourth of July apple pies with stars on the crust.

Remember to think outside the box.

Have you ever heard this expression before? It means to be imaginative and do things differently than everyone else.

I came up with Snap Caps® because I wanted something to decorate my locker with and couldn't find anything I liked. Another way to come up with a good idea is to make something you want, but can't find in stores. It's important to be unique and come up with your own creative ideas.

And watch yo

SNAP CAPS®
by
m3 girl designs LLC

Like a big piece of bubble gum that's about to burst, an original name really sticks with us.

Long before Snap Caps® had their official name, I knew I had to invent something kids would remember. It had to be a fun name, of course, and say something about my product. If you've ever played with Snap Caps®, you know they make a snappy sound when their magnets come together. I was pretty lucky. Snap Caps® almost named themselves! But a good catchy name can take awhile. So don't be in a rush! This creative process is called

BRANDING.

It's filled with possibilities, so be sure to ask the opinions of your family and best friends.

Definition

branding
Naming a product or service in a very clever way so that people will remember it. Branding frequently includes a LOGO design, a symbol that sometimes features a company's name. Take a look at your favorite sneakers and jeans, and you'll see that logos are everywhere.

Originality Rocks!

Ballet Boot Camp

Princess in training

The Party Princess

I ♥ chocolate

Suzie's Fudge-Alicious Brownie Pops

Miss Wonder Weeds

Here are some examples
of fun company names.

The Doll Spa

Patti's Pet Pal

Portraits 2 Go

Bees' Knees Tees

Starting a business all by

yourself can be pretty tricky.

So definitely think of turning to your parents, siblings, BFFs, and

MENTORS

to help you out. They'll advise you.
They'll team up with you.
And because they believe in you,
they'll do all they can to spread the
word about your business.

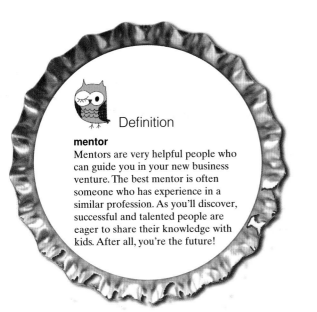

Definition

mentor
Mentors are very helpful people who can guide you in your new business venture. The best mentor is often someone who has experience in a similar profession. As you'll discover, successful and talented people are eager to share their knowledge with kids. After all, you're the future!

A message from Mom:

It's wonderful being a Mom. And it's especially fun when you're helping your daughter start a business. I knew it was important to encourage Maddie to believe in her creative talents. "Think Positive!" is a favorite expression in the Bradshaw family. And that means never be afraid to try something you believe in.

Maddie, Margot and I all help and support each other. And we always feel gratitude for the popularity of Snap Caps® and the happiness we share. I wish you success... and smiles. And always remember to be a kid!

☮ Diane

Margot wants to say:

I'm the Vice President of m3 girl designs. I help my sister come up with new ideas. I get a lot of ideas from my friends and what they like. I love fashion. Eventually, I'll take over the business, start my own line of clothes, and live my dream every day.

XOXO,
Margot ♡

Did somebody say...

Ready for the next big step?

In addition to all the fun stuff like coming up with your business idea and a fabulous name, it's important to get a little more serious when it comes to the subject of **MONEY.**

Lots of paper and plenty of sharpened pencils will come in handy as you figure how much money you'll need to introduce yourself to the neighborhood...the world...the universe!

"Money?"

Important:
Number "crunching" can stir up an appetite, so having something delicious nearby is always a good idea.

EXPENSES

Starting a business is like building a house. It sure helps to have a solid foundation under you. And that means having enough money. Not a trillion dollars (that's $1,000,000,000,000)! Not money for silly things that aren't important. Just enough money to help you start your business and keep it going before your wonderful ideas really catch on.

For example, you'll need to set aside funds for necessary things like these:

✓ Materials and supplies if you're manufacturing a product—the essentials to keep you going for a while (and always purchased at the best possible price)

✓ All the things you'll need for a service business—like gardening tools, paint brushes, exercise weights, even a pooper scooper for dog walkers

✓ Basic office supplies—your own special supply of paper, pens, scissors, a notebook, a calendar, plus a calculator with big numbers that are easy to use

✓ Business cards—you'll impress customers, and they'll remember you

✓ A lawyer and accountant—when your business grows much bigger

✓ And a few other things you may not think of at first

OFFICIAL EXPENSE WORKSHEET

	Cost
Very Important Stuff	
	$
Total:	

	Cost
Less Important Stuff	
	$
	$
Total:	

MY GRAND TOTAL IS:

There's an old saying: "*Money doesn't grow on trees.*"

Guess what? That only happens in our *dreams!*

❀ A sign 20 stories tall

❀ A matching outfit for everyone on my staff

❀ A float in the Macy's Thanksgiving Day Parade

❀ A research trip to Paris

❀ A giant TV to check the weather

❀ A vacation after one month

Get your head out of the clouds. Think smart!

But where do you start?

Hmm, let's see...

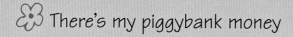

🌸 There's my piggybank money

🌸 Visits from the tooth fairy

🌸 Birthday presents from grandma and grandpa

🌸 Last summer's lemonade stand earnings

🌸 My allowance

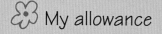

what if you need MORE money?

The money you already have can be
increased with funds from INVESTORS.
These are people who believe in you
and your business ambition.
Investors can be anyone you know.
When your business becomes successful,
you'll be able to pay them back.
You might even add something called

INTEREST.

Definition

interest
Interest is the cost of borrowing
money—the extra amount of dollars
that you pay back to an investor or
a bank, in addition to the amount
of money that was borrowed.

PROFITS:
Your Hard Work Rewarded

The Money You Earn – Your

Business Expenses = Your Profit

I've kept things pretty simple here to give you the basic formula, and simple is the best way to start.

Saving for the Future

Even though you're young, it's smart to think about the future.
Sure, it's tempting to take your profits and buy something
right away, like new sneakers or a really cool bike.
But it's smarter to put your money in the
bank and SAVE FOR SPECIAL GOALS.

What are your dreams?
Maybe you'd love a new computer. Ballet lessons.
A glamourous trip to Europe. Maybe you're
looking way, way ahead to college and
helping out with tuition expenses.
What about a car?

Saving for your future is a wise idea.
(But a few little treats right now are irresistible!)

Giving to Others

Some of your profits can go to your favorite charity.
Charities help people close to home and far away, providing
important things like food, medicine, and shelter.
Each contribution you give—whatever the amount—can
make a big difference.

Giving feels good!
Knowing that we're able to help people, especially kids,
encourages all of us to work even harder.

The smallest kid can from the crowd.

It's also a wise idea to set aside some of your profits to help your business grow and prosper. One of the best ways to do this is to invest in

MARKETING

Definition

marketing
Promoting yourself and your business by spreading the word in all sorts of imaginative and unexpected ways. Smart marketing helps you get noticed.

Guess what? You've got a super story to tell about your business that makes you really special. Start writing.

ADVERTISE WITH IMAGINATION
Wow...your own ad! Make it memorable with a clever headline that will stand out in a local paper... or even taped to a tree.

INTRODUCE YOURSELF TO THE LOCAL RADIO STATION
People love to hear happy news about kids in the business world. Write to your favorite station and ask them to interview you.

WEAR A SILLY COSTUME AND SAY "HI!"
It's okay to look a little goofy. Your goal is to get people's attention and to get them excited about you and your product or service.

CREATE IRRESISTIBLE SPECIAL OFFERS
Everyone loves a deal. Think about offering a tempting discount to first-time customers, or even a "thank you" discount to repeat customers.

A single web page tells a big story, making you look very official.
Think of the interesting story and pictures you'd like to share.

PRINT YOUR OWN BUSINESS CARDS

You can use a home computer and print cards in no time. A local
printer can also show you different paper and design possibilities.

PUT A MESSAGE ON YOUR SCHOOL'S BULLETIN BOARDS

Kids love supporting other kids, especially from the same school.
Make sure your flyer is colorful, with a bold message everyone notices.

Here I am!

stand out

The Absolute Best Part

of my business is visiting stores all around the country and meeting other kids. I love hearing about their ideas and their dreams, and inspiring them to reach their goals. Make sure that whatever you're doing is fun and something you're passionate about!

Being an entrepreneur
can be very exciting!

All of a sudden, you're more than a kid. You're a young professional running a business. You're meeting new people.

You're bursting with confidence and looking ahead to new projects and experiences.

You're an entrepreneur!

YOU CAN DO IT!

We all make a few clumsy mistakes at the beginning.
If at first you don't succeed, keep on trying.

Maybe your first big entrepreneurial adventure
isn't the success you hoped it would be.
Don't be sad. ☺

Take advantage of everything you've learned and the
new friends you've made. Perhaps your business idea
simply needs a little fine-tuning to make it extra
special. Or there's a terrific new marketing idea you'd
like to try. Go for it! The chances are excellent that
you're closer to getting it right than you ever imagined.

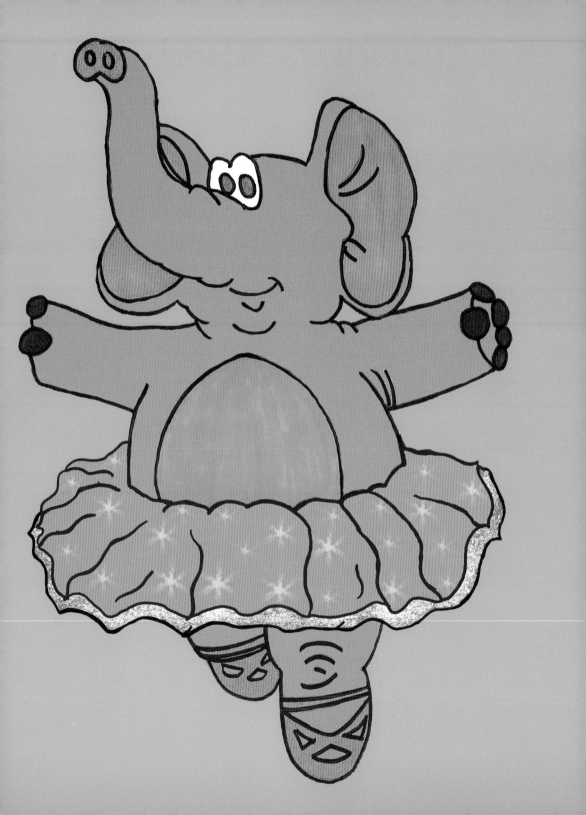

We're all capable of wonderful things.

Inspiring thoughts from the people I admire

"The biggest adventure you can take is
to live the life of your dreams."
—Oprah Winfrey

"The future belongs to those who believe
in the beauty of their dreams."
—Eleanor Roosevelt

"Every great dream begins with a
dreamer. Always remember, you have
within you the strength, the patience,
and the passion to reach for the stars
to change the world."
—Harriet Tubman

"I do not pray for success,
I ask for faithfulness."
—Mother Teresa

"Remember, if you ever need a helping hand, it's at the end of your arm; as you get older, remember you have another: the first is to help yourself, the second is to help others."
—**Audrey Hepburn**

"A girl should be two things: classy and fabulous."
—**Coco Chanel**

"If you don't like something, change it. If you can't change it, change your attitude."—**Maya Angelou**

I can't wait to hear about your entrepreneurial stories.

I hope my book has inspired you to follow your dreams and be successful. When you believe in yourself, who knows what you can accomplish!

I'd love to hear from you!
Send us your success story to:

Maddie
m3 girl designs LLC
PO Box 1263
Addison, TX 75001